THE

DANISH

ART OF

WHITTLING

Simple Projects for the Home

THE
DANISH
ART OF
WHITTLING

Simple Projects for the Home

Frank Egholm

BATSFORD

First published in the United Kingdom in 2018 by
B.T. Batsford
43 Great Ormond Street
London
WC1N 3HZ

An imprint of B.T. Batsford Holdings Ltd

ISBN 9781849945035

A CIP catalogue record for this book is available
from the British Library.

10 9 8
25 24 23 22

Reproduction by Mission Productions, Hong Kong
Printed and bound by Toppan Leefung Printing Ltd, China

This book can be ordered direct from the publisher at
www.batsford.com or try your local bookshop.

CONTENTS

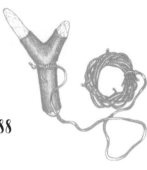

USEFUL THINGS 88

GAMES 128

GETTING STARTED

Read this section to help you choose the best knife and other tools and materials, and to learn the basic techniques that will help you whittle safely.

INTRODUCTION

In recent years there has been a resurgence of interest in the age-old art of whittling, when a knife is used to carve shapes from fresh wood. It's a simple, inexpensive craft that the whole family can get involved in, with parents or grandparents passing on their knowledge to their children, and brothers and sisters helping each other out.

Whittling has many advantages: it is an easy way to create things; it is absorbing; it enables new abilities to be acquired; and it improves concentration, coordination and willpower. People have always enjoyed whittling wood – not only does it promote a combination of different skills, but it's an enjoyable way to pass the time, too, and motivation for getting outside.

In my experience, whittling brings people together in a group where the atmosphere is almost always friendly, encouraging many a cosy chat, which makes it a great activity for families to enjoy together.

Frank Egholm

TOOLS AND SKILLS

The kind of whittling described in this book requires only a few tools, and a wide variety of things can be made with just a knife and a saw. Whether enjoyed as a group or family activity, it is important that you know how to handle a sharp knife safely and that the safety rules are observed at all times, so please read the sections on whittling methods and techniques (see page 23) and the safety rules (see page 37) before making a start on any of the projects.

THE WOOD

Most of the items in this book are carved from fresh branches, which are usually easier to carve than dry wood. I have generally used twigs and small branches with a thickness of 1–4cm (⅜–1½in) from a variety of tree species, such as birch, hazel, cherry, poplar, alder or lime, but other types can also be used. Knotty branches, side branches and nodes can be difficult to work with, but can provide decorative opportunities for the more experienced whittler. If carving patterns in the bark, it is best to choose wood with a nice, smooth bark that is not too thick.

Sometimes you will want to use the wood in which the pith – the spongy centre of the branch – is not too thick (see the projects for advice on this). If you are not lucky enough to have fresh wood available from your garden, ask neighbours or friends if they have some they can spare when pruning, or speak to the gardeners in your local park. Good fresh garden waste can often be found at recycling centres, too.

To avoid cracking, the wood must not dry out too quickly, so store it outside in a cool, dry place. This is also a good way to prevent an unfinished piece from drying out and becoming too hard in between whittling sessions; alternatively, keep an ongoing project in a plastic bag (although not for too long, otherwise it may go mouldy). Soft woods, such as poplar, alder and lime, can be used for pieces that are to be worked on over a longer period. An ideal starter wood for simple projects is dry lime wood as it is so easy to carve.

Above: Learning to whittle helps improve concentration and dexterity. To help avoid accidents, whittlers should never sit within arm's reach of each other.

THE WHITTLING KNIFE

When selecting a whittling knife, here are a few things to look out for:

- Choose a knife with a short blade – a length of 4–7cm (1½–2¾in) is best; some shapes can be difficult to carve if the blade is longer.
- The ideal cutting angle for a whittling knife is 20–25 degrees (see Sharpening the knife, page 28).
- The handle should be comfortable to hold; smaller knives will require smaller handles.

Above: Various whittling knives, some with whittled handles (see page 118).

Above: It's a good idea to keep your knives together in one place.

- A handle that is thicker in the middle and thinner towards each end fits the hand well and provides a good grip.
- For beginners, a knife with a small finger-guard is a good idea, but a large finger-guard of the kind often found on scout knives can get in the way when whittling.

Some suppliers of whittling knives are listed on page 140. If you want to make a whittling knife yourself, these suppliers also sell knife blades, and there are instructions for making a handle and sheath on pages 118–123.

Above: Method 1, cutting away from yourself.

WHITTLING METHODS AND TECHNIQUES

First, read the safety rules on page 37. For extra safety, you may want to protect your hands with cut-resistant protective work gloves.

Cutting away from yourself

The whittling knife must be sharp so it cuts easily and produces a good smooth cut (see Sharpening the knife, page 28). When whittling your mantra should be: 'Always cut away from yourself.' Here are two ways to do this:

METHOD 1: The easiest method is to hold the wood in one hand – the holding hand – and take the knife in your other hand, using it to cut away from you further along the branch. Watch out for your thighs and the fingers of your holding hand. One disadvantage of this method is that the knife moves out into space after leaving the wood, giving you less control over the blade (see the photographs opposite).

METHOD 2: For more controlled and delicate carving, use the thumb of the holding hand to push and support the back of the knife blade; in this way, the knife will make cuts as it is pushed and twisted (see the photographs opposite and below). It can take a little practice to become proficient at this method and the unaccustomed action may make the skin on your thumb a little sore to start with, although the wearing of a thumb guard can help with this.

Small cuts produce neatly finished surfaces – aim to remove small chips of wood at a time. This will produce curves that can be rounded off better when sanding and helps you to get a good feeling for the finished shape while you are carving.

Above and left: Method 2, using both hands to control the knife.

Other cutting tips

When cutting into the wood, cut downhill along the grain of the wood as shown in the illustration below: the arrows on the illustration below show the direction in which the wood should be cut and you should turn the wood as necessary to make sure that you are always cutting away from yourself.

It can be difficult to hold a small piece of wood while whittling it, so you may need to start with a longer branch than required to give you a piece to hold as you whittle. This extra piece can then be sawn off when you have finished (see whittling the bird on the whistle on page 93).

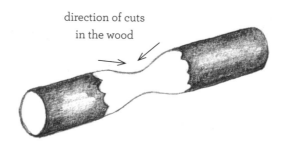

direction of cuts
in the wood

Above: Whittling board.

Alternatively, if there is not much wood to hold while whittling, it can be helpful to prop or support one end of the branch against a tree stump or similar; or you can make a whittling board, a simple seat with an integrated wood support (see the photograph above and the illustration below). Directions for making a whittling board are given in my book, *Snitte: The Danish Art of Whittling*.

Whittling board.

Sharpening the knife

The knife must be sharp in order to be able to cut into the wood, but sharpening is not easy and requires practise. You can use either a sharpening stone to sharpen by hand, or a machine. Sharpening stones are available in various materials and grain sizes: start with a medium or coarse sharpening stone and then move on to a finer one; for a very blunt knife, begin by using a hard-grade Arkansas stone then a fine/ultra-fine ceramic stone or a synthetic diamond whetstone followed by the fine or ultra-fine ceramic stone.

When sharpening by hand, move the knife across the stone in small circular movements or stroke the edge of the blade across the stone (see the photograph, opposite). It is important to hold the knife at an angle to the stone to produce an edge angle of 20–25 degrees on each side of the knife. You can make your own angle measure from a piece of cardboard or plywood (see diagram below).

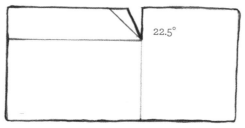

Cutting-angle measure.

Water-cooled knife sharpening machines are also available, in which a whetstone spins around on a wheel while water runs over it. These are efficient sharpeners and the water prevents the blade from overheating (too much heat will turn the steel blue and spoil the hardening so making it brittle). Some machines will have a rotating leather disc for the final sharpening, otherwise this must be done by hand.

Splitting wood

To make some of the projects, it will be necessary to split a branch. For example, to make a butter knife (see page 98) you need to start with a small wedge-shaped piece of wood.

Wood can be split in a controlled way by placing the edge of the axe-blade on the place where the wood is to be split and then striking the back of the axe-head with a wooden mallet or piece of wood – never use a metal hammer or tool for this job. Split the wood in half first, then in quarters, and continue until you have obtained the thickness you want.

To split small branches, use a knife instead of an axe, and use another branch to strike the back of the knife-blade as shown left.

Smoothing wood

The wood needs to dry for a few days before sanding or oiling. The surface of whittled wood can be finely shaped or smoothed using sandpaper of different grit sizes – the higher the grit size the finer the paper. Start with coarse sandpaper (low grit numbers, 80–100) and carry on using increasingly fine sandpaper (I have recommended up to 240, but if you prefer a completely smooth surface, you can use even finer sandpapers than indicated in the projects – grit numbers 320–1000).

Note: if the sanded wood gets damp, it will become rough due to the wood fibres springing up from the surface, so it is important to finish the whittled project after sanding with a surface treatment to make it moisture repellent (see finishing, opposite).

Decorating

Some whittled pieces can be coloured with watercolour paints, preferably thinned sufficiently that the woodgrain can still be seen through the paint. Once the paint is dry, apply a coating of linseed oil (see finishing, below).

Finishing

A surface treatment should be applied to protect and seal a whittled piece and I generally use linseed oil applied with a cloth (the wood can be made more moisture repellent by rubbing the liquid oil in with a fine sandpaper) See box, page 34.

Raw, cold-pressed linseed oil is a very pure oil that penetrates deep into the wood but takes a long time to dry; other types are available that are less pure, containing additives that reduce the drying time.

Wooden utensils such as the butter knives (see page 98) should be finished with food-safe medicinal-grade liquid paraffin (mineral) oil.

Caution: When using linseed oil, always read and follow the manufacturer's instructions.

Work in a well-ventilated area, preferably outside, and keep well away from fire or naked flames. Cloths soaked in linseed oil may ignite spontaneously, so immediately after use, place the cloths in a bucket of water outdoors.

Hand-wash with detergent to remove all traces of oil, rinsing and repeating as necessary, then air dry. Cleaned cloths should be kept in a tightly closed metal container or disposed of safely.

TOOLS AND EQUIPMENT

Here is a list of items I used to make the projects in this book. For specific project requirements, see the materials list alongside each project.

- Whittling knife.
- Saw.
- Hand or electric drill with wood drill bits of various sizes.
- Auger: a hand tool with a bit shaped like a corkscrew for boring larger holes.
- Gimlet: a screw-tipped hand tool for boring smaller holes.
- Bradawl: painted tool used to make a neat hole or indentation in wood.
- Axe.
- Hammer.
- Wooden mallet.
- Sandpaper of various grit numbers.
- Linseed oil and cloth to apply it with.
- Scissors.
- String and cord.
- Screws and nails.
- Watercolour paints; leather paint; paintbrushes.
- Glues: wood; hobby; two-part epoxy adhesive (for sticking wood to other materials such as metal).
- Dowelling in various sizes: 5mm, 6mm, 8mm, 10mm, 13mm.

STAYING SAFE

When working with whittling knives and other woodworking tools such as drills and saws, safety is paramount. Protective gloves are advisable, particularly on the hand holding the wood. An adult should always supervise children, ensuring that they observe the key safety rules listed below, and you should make sure a well-stocked first-aid box is kept close to hand.

Safety rules
- Always sit down when whittling.
- Keep at a distance from others and make sure anyone sitting near you keeps at a distance, too.
- Cut away from yourself. Be especially careful about your thighs and the hand holding the knife.
- Hold the knife close to the item you are whittling. Never point or gesticulate when you have a knife in your hand.
- Keep the knife in its sheath when it is not being used or when handing it to others. Instructions for making a sheath are given on pages 121–123.
- Never walk around with an unsheathed knife.

TOYS

· · · · · · · ·

This range of toys starts simple and
becomes more and more challenging,
so there is something for every ability.

SWORD AND SABRE

Swords and sabres turn children into great and powerful warriors, but of course they must be used with care! They are simple projects for beginners, giving plenty of opportunity to practise removing bark and whittling wood to a point at the end of the 'blade'.

SWORD

Materials

- Fresh branch, 40–60cm (15½–23½in) long and 2–3cm (¾–1⅛in) thick.
- Fresh branch, 15–20cm (6–8in) long and 1.5–2.5cm (⅝–1in) thick.
- Sandpaper, grit number 80–240 (optional).
- String.
- Silver or gold paint and paintbrush (optional).
- Acrylic gems and two-part epoxy adhesive (optional).

I. Remove the bark from the longer branch (if you prefer, you can leave some bark in place for the handle grip). Sharpen the branch to a point at one end and round off the other (handle) end. Take the shorter branch (this will become the handle cross-guard) and round it off at both ends. Remove the bark or leave it on as you prefer. If you wish, you can sand the whittled surfaces of the branches smooth with sandpaper.

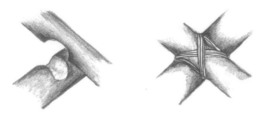

2. Cut a notch in both branches at the point where they
will cross (see the illustration above left). Tie the two
pieces together in a cross-shape with the string (see the
illustration above right). To develop your embellishing
skills, make a 'metal' sword by painting the 'blade' with
silver or gold paint, and decorate the hilt by gluing on
acrylic gems.

SABRE

Materials

- Fresh branch, 40–60cm (15½–23½in) long and 2–3cm (¾–1⅛in) thick.
- Auger, 5–10mm.
- Piece of willow, 15–20cm (6–8in) long and 5–10mm (¼–⅜in) thick.
- Sandpaper, grit number 80–240 (optional).

....

1. Remove the bark from the part of the branch that will form the blade, leaving the bark on the part that will form the handle. Cut the branch to a point at the end of the stripped section and round off the handle end; sand the whittled surfaces smooth if you choose to.

2. Use the auger to bore a hole at each end of the handle section, halfway into the wood and at a slight angle, so that when you insert the ends of the willow twig they are held in place by the pressure (see the illustration below).

RING CATCHER

The basic ring catcher is a very easy project for those who have not had much whittling practice. Those looking to develop their carving skills can make a more ornate stop branch (see the photograph opposite).

Materials

- Fresh forked branch, 15–20cm (6–8in) long, with a handle section about 8–10cm (3⅛–4in) long, 2–3cm (¾–1⅛in) thick; the fork that catches the ring (the catching branch) should be about 8cm (3⅛in) long, while the stop branch (which stops the ring slipping down onto the handle) need only be about 4–5cm (1½–2in) long.
- Sandpaper, grit number 80–240 (optional).
- Hand or electric drill with 3–4mm drill bit (optional).
- Watercolour paint and paintbrush (optional).
- String.
- Thin, flexible willow branch or birch twigs, 30–40cm (12–16in) long, to make the ring.

1. Whittle the catching branch to a point and round off the other two ends of the branch, leaving the bark on the sections in between (see the illustration below). For a slightly more complex project, you can cut patterns into the bark or remove it completely.

Note: the bark is difficult to cut away where the branch forks, so great care should be taken to avoid an accident.

2. The ring catcher can be made more ornate by carving the stop branch into a bird (see page 82), or you could paint a face on it and turn the catching branch into a long nose (see pages 96–97), or you could carve a small elf at one end of it (see pages 66–71).

3. When you have finished carving the ring catcher you can sand the whittled areas smooth with sandpaper and paint them with thinned watercolour paint.

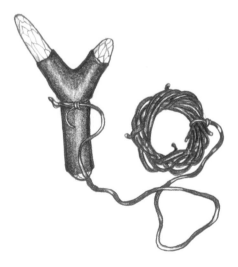

4. Just below the fork, either cut a groove all the way around the branch to create a shallow channel for the string to sit in, or drill a hole right the way through it, and tie one end of a length of string in place.

5. Now make the ring to tie on to the other end of the string by weaving the willow branch or birch twigs into a circle. (You many need to wind an extra branch or twig around the circle to give it added weight, to make it easier to throw the ring into the air.) Tie the completed ring to the other end of the string.

6. Hold the ring catcher with one hand and swing the ring up into the air. Then all you have to do is catch it!

MAGIC PROPELLER

Here's a great trick for budding conjurors – a propeller that can turn to the right or the left at your command!

Materials
- Small fresh branch, 30–40cm (12–16in) long and 1–1.6cm (³⁄₈–⁵⁄₈in) thick: the middle 10–15cm (4–6in) of the branch must be straight, with no side branches and preferably no knots. The wood you choose should not have a thick pith as this will dampen the vibrations; hazel is very suitable.
- A piece of fresh branch for the propeller, about 10cm (4in) long and 1–2cm (³⁄₈–³⁄₄in) thick.
- Small fresh branch, 15–20cm (6–8in) long and 5–10mm (¹⁄₄–³⁄₈in) thick.
- Gimlet, 1.5–2mm.
- Round nail with 1.5mm head.
- Saw.

saw off

1. Take the longest branch and cut 8–10 notches in its middle section at intervals of 1–1.5cm (³⁄₈–⁵⁄₈in), cutting about one-third of the way into the branch (see the illustration below left). Cut from each side alternately and take care not to break off any wood in between the notches – if you do break the wood, start again with a new branch. Once you have whittled the notches, saw off the holding piece at one end of the stick and neaten the ends (see the illustration below left).

2. Split the smallest branch (see splitting wood, page 31) to make a small flat propeller about 4–5cm (1½–2in) in length, making sure to carve the pith from the inner edge and sawing off any surplus. Using the gimlet, bore a hole in the centre of the propeller and mount it on the nail. Balance the propeller by whittling away the wood where it is too heavy, then fix the propeller to the end of the notched branch by pushing down the nail into the pith of the notched stick.

3. Take the remaining branch and neaten the ends. This is the tool with which you will operate the propeller stick as described below, and the bark can be left on and decorated with patterns, or it can be removed completely (see the photographs below and opposite).

4. And now for the magic. Hold the propeller stick horizontally and run the smaller stick back and forth over the notches. The propeller will spin around without being touched.

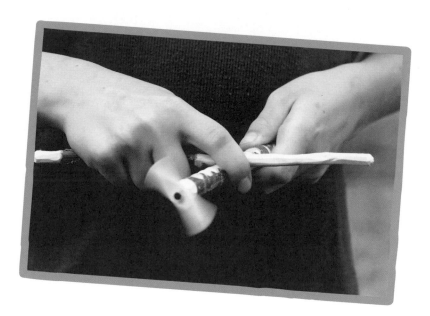

Tell your audience that the propeller will change
direction magically if asked politely or in response
to a whistle, for example. They won't notice that it
is your finger position that is making the propeller
change direction.

Mostly you can make the propeller turn one way or
another by pressing either the right or left side of
the propeller stick with one finger, while running
the other stick over the notches.

WINDMILL

The windmill has sailboards that really
turn and it is a nice easy project.

Materials
- Piece of fresh branch for the mill, 6–8cm (2⅜–3⅛in) long and
3–4cm (1⅛–1½in) thick.
- Piece of fresh branch for the sails, about 15cm (6in) long and 1–2cm
(⅜–¾in) thick (preferably wood that does not have too much pith).
- Piece of 5mm dowelling, 7–10cm (2¾–4in) long.
- Hand or electric drill with 5mm and 6mm drill bits.
- Sandpaper: grit number 80–240 (optional).
- Linseed oil (optional).
- Wood glue.

....

1. Round off the top of the branch for the mill with small,
delicate cuts to give you an even dome – this can be
difficult to carve, so take extra care not to cut your index
finger. The rest of the bark can be left on, or it can be
removed completely and sanded smooth with sandpaper.

2. To make two small boards for the sails, start by splitting
the branch for the sails lengthways (see page 31). Whittle
the boards until they are flat, carving the inner side first
and removing the pith: each of the sails should be about
1.5cm (⅝in) wide and 5–7cm (2–2¾in) long and look
identical. Drill a 5mm hole in the centre of each sail.

3. To attach the sails to complete the windmill, start by either neatly whittling or sanding smooth the ends of the length of dowelling (you can give the sails and dowelling a coating of linseed oil before continuing if you wish). Place one sail on top of the other in a cross-shape then push it onto one end of the dowelling, using a little wood glue to fix together. Now drill a 6mm hole all the way through the centre of the domed top of the mill. The dowelling is threaded through the top of the windmill so that the sails are at the front and a piece of the dowelling pokes out at the back to give you a handle to turn to make the sails move around.

FLYING PROPELLER

The propeller is a fun toy – for grown-ups and children – but it requires a certain degree of control when whittling.

Materials
- Strip of wood for the propeller, 11–13cm (4¼–5in) long, 2–2.5cm (¾–1in) wide and 8–10mm (⁵⁄₁₆–³⁄₈in) thick: I chose a light, easy-to-carve dry lime wood, but a fresh, light wood such as lime or willow works too.
- Auger, 5mm.
- 5mm dowelling for the launch handle, about 10cm (4in) long.

• •

1. Using the auger, bore a hole in the centre of one of the long sides of the wood strip (to house the launch handle). Carve the propeller blades to either side of the hole, cutting each half obliquely between top and bottom edge, making sure the blades slope in different directions. Turn the propeller over and repeat on the other side of the wood – it may help to draw on where the wood should be cut away. The blades must be cut as thin as possible, so the propeller will be very light.

Note: it may be difficult to make the blades thin close to the centre of the propeller without carving too much off the ends.

2. To balance the propeller, insert the dowelling launch handle in the hole and lay it on the table so that the propeller hangs over the table edge. Hold the dowelling lightly, so that if one side of the propeller is heavier it will drop down, and cut away the wood until the whole thing is balanced.

3. To make the propeller fly, hold the launch handle between your hands as shown on page 54. Rub the rod between your palms quickly so that the propeller rotates and rises to float up in the air as your hands separate. If the propeller dive bombs, try twirling it between your hands again, this time rubbing the rod in the other direction. (If the propeller does not spin evenly it may be because it is not properly balanced or because the dowelling is too light in relation to the propeller.)

BUZZING WHIRLIGIG

The name of this simple toy comes from the buzzing or whistling sound produced when the whirligig spins around quickly, first in one direction and then the other.

Materials
- Fresh branch, about 15cm (6in) long and 1.5–2cm (⅝–¾in) thick.
- Gimlet, 2–3mm.
- Thin string, e.g. knotting cord or nylon line, about 1m (1yd) long.
- Two pieces of fresh branch for the handles, about 5cm (2in) long and 5–10mm (¼–⅜in) thick.
- Darning needle (optional).

1. Carve out a curved depression all the way around the middle of the branch: it should be thinner in the centre and about 2.5cm (1in) long (see the illustration below). See page 26 for more on how to do this. Saw off one end of the branch about 1cm (⅜in) from the carved middle section and round the end off. Repeat at the other end.

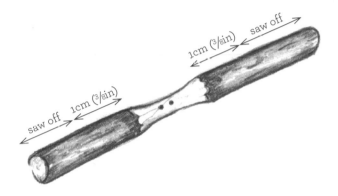

2. Using the gimlet, bore two holes through the carved middle section about 1cm (⅜in) apart. Thread the string through the holes (it may help to use a darning needle) and tie the ends of the string together.

3. Position the whirligig in the middle of the strings and tie or fix the handles to the ends of the string (see the illustrations below and opposite).

4. Now you are ready to test the whirligig. To wind up the string, keep hold of the handles and twirl the whirligig around about 10–12 times, keeping the string loose. Then slowly pull the string tight and the whirligig will spin around. When the string begins to wind back on itself again, slacken the string a little and when it has gone round as far as it can, pull it tight again. It is important to get into a good rhythm, so that the whirligig will spin quickly first one way and then the other.

Note: Interestingly, a whirligig made from fresh wood will spray out sap the first few times it spins as a result of centrifugal force.

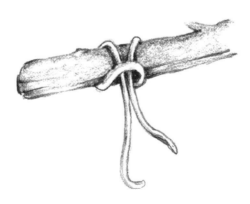

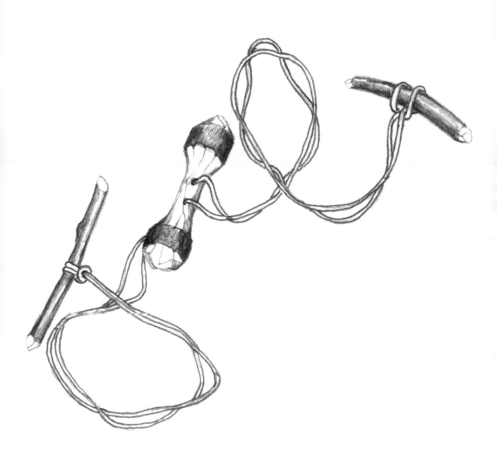

SOMERSAULTING BEAR

Tip this bear onto its forelegs to see it tumble forwards.
This is a great introduction to more detailed carving.

Materials
- Block of wood, 7.5cm (3in) long (in the direction of the grain of the wood), 4.5cm (1¾in) high and 4cm (1½in) wide. Juniper wood will give the bear a beautiful dark colour, as shown in the photograph below.
- Linseed oil.

1. Carve the outline of the bear as seen from the side (see the illustration below) and begin to shape it a little. Review the shape as you work, and keep whittling until you are satisfied. Placed on a flat surface, the bear should turn a somersault when it is tipped over just beyond its point of balance on its forelegs.

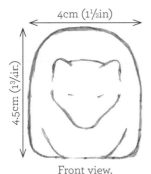

4cm (1½in)

4.5cm (1¾in)

Front view.

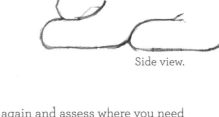

7.5cm (3in)

4.5cm (1¾in)

Side view.

2. Check the shape again and assess where you need to make any further cuts. Is the rear end too heavy? Or should a little bit be taken off the ears so that the bear will somersault correctly?

3. Finish carving the head and legs of the bear. Both ears should protrude forwards by the same distance and the bear's back should be slightly flat so that it will not roll to one side. Check every now and then as you continue to carve that the bear can still turn somersaults. If you find that some parts are difficult to carve, try clamping the bear to a workbench and use a small gouge. Give the bear a coat of linseed oil to finish (see page 33–34).

FIGURES AND ANIMALS

Figures are fun and surprisingly easy to carve, and you can give them character with some paint and a little imagination. Or take advantage of the natural shape of the wood to make a mouse, a bear or a bird.

ELF 1

The basic elf is a charming small project for beginners.
Elves like company, so why not make several – after all,
practice makes perfect.

Materials

- Piece of fresh branch, 5–8cm (2–3⅛in) long plus an extra 5cm (2in)
  to hold while whittling, 1–3cm (⅜–1⅛in) thick (choose one with an
  attractive but not too thick bark).
- Saw.
- Pencil.
- Beeswax crayon, coloured pencil or watercolour paint
  and paintbrush.

Above: If Elf 1 seems too simple, try Elf 2 (see page 68).

1. Cut the tip of the branch to a point like a pencil but leave the bark on the rest of the length (it's a good idea to have another piece of fresh branch ready for a second attempt in case you remove too much bark). Carve the beard and face by removing a little more of the bark (see the illustrations left).

2. Saw off the holding end of the branch so that your elf is the required height. Mark the eyes and mouth with a pencil: two dots and a small curving line.

3. The hat can be coloured with thinned watercolour paint, beeswax crayon or coloured pencil.

ELF 2

Another elf design – this one is a great introduction to carving a shaped form.

Materials

· Piece of fresh branch, 15–20cm (6–8in) long (includes extra to hold while whittling) and 2–4cm (¾–1½in) thick.
· Saw.
· Sandpaper, grit number 80–240 (optional).
· Watercolour paints and paintbrush.
· Linseed oil (optional).

1. Carve the elf in the middle of the branch (this makes it easier to carve all the way around), cutting in at the neck to make the head of the elf and shaping the hat (see the photograph, right). You can either leave the bark on the elf's body intact or remove it as you choose. See page 26 for advice on cutting.

2. Once you have finished carving the elf, cut the hat free from the holding piece, then saw off the other end of the branch to the required length. You can sand the elf to finish, then paint in his features and colour his tunic and hat – red is a good choice for a Christmas elf. Finish with the linseed oil if you wish (see pages 33–34).

FIGURES

Who is your figure going to be? Maybe it is you,
a family member or even a fantasy character.

1. Carve a round ball-shaped head in the middle of the
branch (see Elf 2, page 68), then saw off the end of
the branch at the very top of the head.

2. Finish by sanding the figure smooth with the sandpaper
if you wish (see the illustrations below), then colour it
with watercolour paints and treat with oil once the paint
has dried (see pages 33–34).

Above: Whittling figures is so much fun, you'll want to make a whole family.

ANGELS

Materials

- Piece of fresh branch, about 10cm (4in) long plus an extra length to hold while whittling, 2.5–3cm (1–1⅛in) thick.
- Sandpaper, grit number 80–240 (optional).
- Watercolour paints and paintbrush.
- Linseed oil.

Additional materials for angel with halo:

- 1mm wire (preferably bronze).
- Thin gimlet to match the thickness of the wire.

Additional materials for angel with wings:

- Piece of fresh branch for wings, 10–15cm (4–6in) long and about 4cm (1½in) thick.
- Saw.
- Hand or electric drill with 5mm drill bit.
- Wood glue.

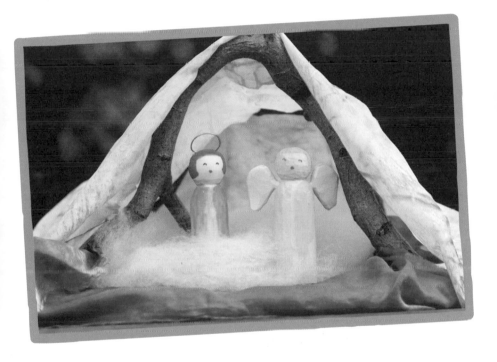

ANGEL WITH HALO

1. Create a basic body shape by following the instructions to make a figure on page 72.

2. Shape the halo from the wire. Using the gimlet, bore a hole at the top of the back of the angel's head and fix the end of the wire firmly in the hole.

ANGEL WITH WINGS

1. Split the branch for the wings down the middle (see page 31). Take one half and carve it flat, to a thickness of about 5mm (¼in), taking care to cut away the pith. Draw two wings in the centre of the flat piece of wood (see the illustration below).

2. The wings are carved as one piece before being sawn apart where the edges of the wings are joined; carve a round peg about 5mm (¼in) thick on each wing to fix it in place. Finally, saw the wings apart and finish the carving along the edge where they were joined.

3. Use the drill to bore holes in the angel's shoulders and glue the wings in place (see the photograph, page 75).

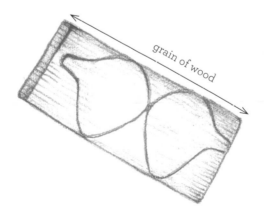

grain of wood

MOUSE

The mouse is a nice easy project for beginners. A whole family can be created to give you lots of whittling practice.

Materials

- Fresh branch, 6–10cm (2⅜–4in) long plus extra length to hold while whittling, 2.5–3cm (1–1⅛in) thick.
- Sandpaper, grit number 80–240 (optional).
- Linseed oil.
- A small piece of thin leather for the ears and tail.
- Gimlet or bradawl.
- Two-part epoxy adhesive.

1. Carve the underside of the branch flat to the length of the mouse so it will stand firmly. Remove the bark along the length of the mouse (or leave it in place) and carve one end with the nose pointing downwards (it may make this easier if the branch has been sawn diagonally). Start to round off the tail end of the mouse, then saw it right off the branch.

2. Leave the surface of the mouse as it has been carved or smooth it with sandpaper if you wish. Coat the mouse with oil (see pages 33–34).

3. Cut out two teardrop shapes from the leather for the ears and a long thin tail also.

4. Use a gimlet or bradawl to bore holes for the ears on top of the head and a hole in the rounded end for the tail. This is tricky; take care to ensure that the gimlet does not slip down into your hand – either hold it close to the tip or clamp the mouse in place.

5. Put a little glue in each of the holes and use a nail or something similar to push the ears and the tail in place. Allow plenty of time for the glue to dry before playing with the mouse.

BEAR

This figure requires precise carving to leave bark in place for the bear's nose and limbs. The best time to carve the bear is in autumn or winter, since in spring and summer the bark of the branch may be too loose.

Materials
- Piece of fresh branch, 6–10cm (2⅜–4in) long plus an optional extra 5cm (2in) to hold while whittling, 2.5–3cm (1–1⅛in) thick (the bark should be attractive and not too thick – hazel is a good option).

. . . .

1. First, carve a dome shape to form the top of the head, and remove the bark from the rest of the head, except for where the nose will be. Carve the muzzle so that it is slightly pointed.

2. Create the limbs by leaving the bark in place as you carve (see the photograph opposite). Finally, carve two small ears, if you wish.

BIRD

Whittle a forked branch into a charming little bird.

Materials
- Fresh forked branch: main branch 5–10cm (2–4in) long and about 2cm (¾in) thick; the part of the branch for the head should be about 3cm (1⅛in) long and the part for the tail, 3–5cm (1⅛–2in) long.
- Saw.

Carve the bird following the illustration below, leaving a piece of bark intact on either side to form the wings. Saw off the branch at the base of the bird when you have finished carving to create a stand.

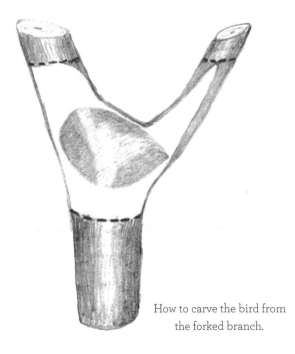

How to carve the bird from
the forked branch.

MARY AND JOSEPH

A nativity scene is a wonderful project. Here are Mary and Joseph, and you can add an angel (see pages 74-77) and make basic figures for shepherds or kings (see pages 72-73).

Materials for each figure

Option 1
- A block of dry lime wood 4 x 4cm (1½ x 1½in), about 10cm (4in) long plus an optional extra 6–8cm (2⅜–3⅛in) to hold while whittling. The corners can be planed off to make the block more comfortable to hold. (The advantage of dry lime wood is that it is easy to carve and does not harden if the piece is worked over a longer period; the disadvantage is that the shape of the block does not relate to the desired figure.)

Option 2
- A fresh branch, about 10cm (4in) long plus an optional extra 6–8cm (2⅜–3⅛in) to hold while whittling, about 4cm (1½) thick. (The advantage of the fresh branch is that it is round like the figure and comfortable to hold; the disadvantages are that the wood will harden and there is a risk of it splitting when it dries.)

Additional materials:
- Sandpaper, grit number 80–240 (optional).
- Linseed oil (optional).
- Gimlet (for Joseph).
- A suitably curved twig, for Joseph's staff.

MARY

1. Round off the top of the head and cut away a little at the back, so that Mary is bending forward slightly (see side view, below).

2. Cut in around the neck, breast and under the arms.

3. Make the sides of the head a little narrower to emphasize the shoulders (see front view, below), taking care not to cut away too much, as the head can easily become too small or too pointed.

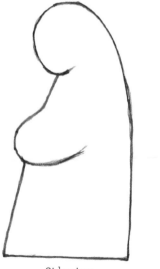

Side view.

Front view.

4. Ask someone to pose for you, so you can see how the length and position of the arms should be in relation to the body. Make sure the face is further forward than the breast but not as far as the arms.

5. The surface can be left showing small fine whittling marks or it can be finished with sandpaper. Lastly, give the figure a coat of linseed oil (see pages 33–34).

JOSEPH

1. Work the figure in the same way as described for Mary.

2. Make sure that one hand and arm protrude far enough from the body to enable you to bore a hole for Joseph's staff. The other arm can hang down beside the body.

3. Note that the body is usually wider than it is deep.

Above: A nativity scene makes a wonderful Christmas gift.

USEFUL THINGS

· · · · · · · ·

From the unquestionably useful coat hooks,
whistles, buttons and knife handles to the
more decorative beads, pendants and flowers,
this section has it all.

WHISTLES

WHISTLE I

Materials

- Piece of straight fresh branch for the whistle, about 12cm (4¾in) long and about 3cm (1⅛in) thick.
- Piece of fresh branch for the bird, 12–14cm (4¾ x 5½in) long (includes extra to hold while whittling) and 1.5–2.5cm (⅝–1in) thick.
- Piece of 13mm dowelling, 3–4cm (1⅛–1½in) long.
- Small piece of 5mm dowelling.
- Hand or electric drill with 5mm and 13mm drill bits (I've used a pillar drill).
- Wood glue.
- Saw.

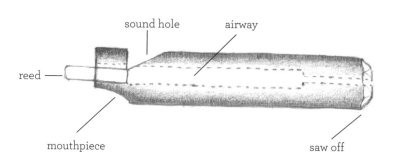

reed — / sound hole / airway / mouthpiece / saw off

1. Drill a 13mm hole about 8–10cm (3⅛–4in) deep in one end (the blowing end) of the whistle branch. Drill a 5mm hole in the other end of the whistle branch, to create an airway running all the way through (see the illustration, left). (I drill the airway channel using a pillar drill before I begin whittling as it is too difficult for beginners to do safely.)

2. Using your knife or a saw, cut a wedge-shaped sound hole near the blowing end of the whistle, first making the straight cut about 1.5cm (⅝in) from the end and deep enough to intersect with the airway (see the illustration, left), then cutting diagonally as shown.

3. Now make a reed using the piece of 13mm dowelling. Cut away 1–2mm from the long edge of the dowelling so it is flat on one side. Insert it into the hole at the blowing end so that the cut-away part is facing upwards and the end of the dowelling aligns with the straight edge of the sound hole (see the illustration on page 90).

4. When blown, your whistle should now make a noise: test it to see, but take care as the reed is still loose at this stage. If you start with a narrow airway and a small sound hole, you can make adjustments by making the holes larger so that the instrument can produce a whistle. (The holes must be cleanly carved.) The position of the dowelling reed may need adjustment to get the best sound (if the dowelling is difficult to pull out, try pushing it out from the inside with even narrower dowelling or similar). Also test whether it makes a difference if you hold your finger over the hole at the other end of the whistle. Once the whistle is working to your liking, glue the dowelling in place for safety and saw off the surplus, level with the end of the wood.

5. Shape the blowing end of the whistle so that it feels comfortable between your lips (see the illustration on page 90). Round off the other end neatly and cut patterns in the bark as desired.

6. Now take the remaining branch and carve the bird following the diagrams below and referring to the photograph on page 91, leaving the bark intact to form the wings.

Note: The diagrams show the bird in the process of being carved and before the extra length has been sawn off. Carve the front of the body first and then the tail: the bird should measure about 7–8cm (2¾–3⅛in). Carving such a small piece is difficult, so support the branch against something (see page 27). Once you are happy with the bird shape, saw off the holding piece and finish carving the tail.

1. Bore a 5mm hole in the middle of the underside of the bird and insert the small piece of 5mm dowelling, sawing it off to leave about 5mm (¼in) protruding. Bore another hole the same size in the top of the whistle and insert the dowelling to fix the bird in place (see the photograph on page 91).

saw here
/

The bird seen from the side.

The bird seen from above.

WHISTLE 2

- Fresh forked branch: main branch, about 10cm (4in) long and about 2.5cm (1in) thick; side branch for the bird's head, about 3cm (1⅛in) long; side branch for the bird's tail/whistle, 8–10cm (3⅛–4in) long and 1.5–2cm (⅝–¾in) thick.
- Hand or electric drill with 8mm or 10mm drill bit.
- 8mm or 10mm dowelling, 2–3cm (¾–1⅛in) long.
- Saw.

● ●

1. Drill a hole about 5cm (2in) into the side branch that forms the tail/whistle. Carve a sound hole (see pages 90–91) and continue working the wood until the parts of the whistle have been completed as for Whistle 1, this time making a reed from the 8mm or 10mm dowelling.

2. Carve the bird's head and leave some bark intact to shape into wings as shown in the photograph opposite. Trim the bottom so your whistle bird can stand up.

HOOK

This hook can be carved to resemble a face, with the nose as the peg, or it can be carved and finished more plainly and sanded smooth if you prefer. If your branch has two or more side branches, you can make a plain hook with more than one peg.

Materials
- Piece of fresh branch with side branch(es) or a forked branch with the side branch in the centre, 10–15cm (4–6in) long plus extra to hold while whittling.
- Saw or axe.
- Sandpaper, grit number 80–240 (optional).
- Watercolour paints and paintbrush (optional).
- Linseed oil (optional).
- Hand or electric drill with 4mm drill bit.
- One or two screws to attach hook to wall.

. . . .

1. Use one of the following methods to remove the back of the branch so that the hook will lie flat against the wall:

Method 1: If the branch is straight, you can use the splitting technique (see page 31).
Method 2: Saw off the back, making sure it is straight (the branch must be longer than the given measurements so that you can use the extra to clamp it in place if using a hand saw, or to hold it if using a band saw).
Method 3: Carve the back flat.

2. Remove the bark, taking great care not to cut yourself when carving where the branches fork. Carve the hook following the photos for inspiration. Once you have finished carving, you can smooth the wood with sandpaper if you wish. Paint a jolly face and add a hat (see below), then finish with a coat of oil (see pages 33–34).

3. Drill the holes for the screws, one at the top and perhaps another at the bottom. If you don't want the screws to be visible, you could position the hook so that it can be screwed in place from the other side of the item it is being fixed to.

BUTTER KNIVES

Two butter knives to whittle from wood. On the first only
the blade is shaped and for the second the whole of the
knife is carved.

BUTTER KNIFE 1

Materials

- Piece of fresh branch with attractive bark of a suitable length
  for a butter knife – about 20cm (8in) – and a thickness that
  is comfortable to hold – about 2.5cm (1in).
- Sandpaper, grit number 80–240 (optional).
- Liquid paraffin (see finishing, pages 33–34).

1. Carve the top half of the branch flat, whittling first on
one side and then the other, shaping the blade as you go.
Make the blade thinner towards the edge but take care
not to make it so thin in the centre of the blade that the
spongy pith shows.

2. Retain the bark on the handle, and cut patterns in it if you wish. Round off the end of the handle. Finish by sanding the knife smooth with sandpaper if you choose to (see page 32), and oil it with liquid paraffin (see pages 33–34).

BUTTER KNIFE 2

Materials

- Piece of fresh branch split into a wedge shape of a suitable length for a butter knife: about 20cm (8in) long and at least 10cm (4in) thick.
- Sandpaper, grit number 100–240 (optional).
- Liquid paraffin (see finishing, pages 33–34).

1. Having split a fresh branch into wedge-shaped pieces (see page 31), first along its length and then along its width if necessary, draw the shape of the knife onto one of the pieces of wood. Draw the blade section at the narrowest end of the wedge.

Tip: If you need to finish the knife another time, put it in a plastic bag with the shavings and leave it somewhere cool to help prevent it drying out.

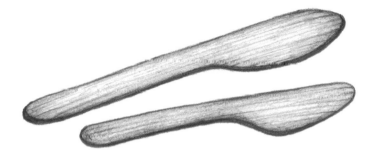

2. Carve the knife to the right shape and thickness (see the illustration above) following the grain of the wood. (It may make it easier to carve if you saw away the wood almost to the bottom of the groove at the base of the blade.) The whittled knife can be sanded smooth with sandpaper if you wish (see page 32), but let the wood dry out first for a few days at room temperature.

3. Oil the knife with food-safe liquid paraffin; if you want to make the utensil more moisture-repellent, apply the oil with fine sandpaper (see page 33).

HIKING POLE

This project requires quite a bit of space in which to work.
It is good for practising whittling patterns in bark.

Materials
· Straight fresh branch, such as a hazel branch, the length of a hiking
pole: the branch should have attractive bark, with no side branches,
and preferably not too many inconvenient knots.

. . . .

1. Carve a decorative shape at the top of the branch, such
as a ball or a figure (see cork decorations, page 117, for
some ideas).

2. Carve patterns in the bark, making sure you cut deep
enough to remove the underbark (the inner layer of
bark). Remember always to cut away from yourself, so
if you are cutting a symmetrical pattern, you may need
to turn the pole around to ensure you are not cutting
towards yourself. (You can place a mat on the ground
so the decorative top will not get dirty in this instance.)

BEADS

Make several beads from one small branch, then thread one or more onto a leather cord and knot the ends together to make a simple necklace.

Materials
- Small fresh branch, about 30cm (12in) long and 2.5–3.5cm (1–1³/₈in) thick.
- Sandpaper, grit number 80–240 (optional).
- Hand or electric drill with 3mm drill bit.
- 1–1.5mm leather cord, 70–90cm (28–35in) long (optional).

1. Carve the first bead in the centre of the branch by cutting away at either side of it (see the illustration, below and page 26). Carve the bead neatly to the desired shape, stripping the bark away or not as you choose. Continue to carve beads along the branch, incising patterns into the bark if you wish. Sand any of the beads smooth, if you choose to, before cutting them free from each other.

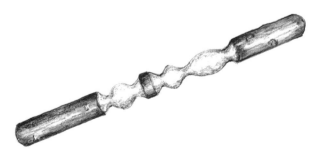

2. Now, starting from one end, drill threading holes through the centre of the beads, ready to thread them on to the leather cord. To make a necklace with an adjustable sliding knot, see page 114.

BUTTONS

Wooden buttons look great on hand-knitted jumpers or used as eyes for handmade soft toys, but you must be sure to sew them on very tightly. They can be quite fiddly to make!

Materials
- Fresh branch, 10–20cm (4–8in) long and 2–4cm (¾–1½) thick (use strong wood with an interesting grain, such as juniper, yew or laburnum – willow, aspen and lime are not suitable).
- Saw, preferably with fine teeth.
- Hand or electric drill with 2–3mm wood drill bit, depending on the size of the button (although a dowel drill bit will be safer and more accurate).
- Sandpaper, grit number 80–240.
- Linseed oil.

1. Remove the bark from the very end of the branch and shape the end so that it is slightly rounded. Whittling at the end of a branch is tricky – you risk getting cut, so be careful that the index finger of your holding hand is kept out of the way of the knife blade. Use whittling method 2, page 25, and whittle carefully using small cuts; try carving at a slight angle instead of straight on.

2. Saw off the button carefully from the end of the branch, as it could easily break. It should be about 5mm (¼in) thick. Drill two holes in the centre of the button. Sand

the back of the button smooth with sandpaper if
you wish. Lightly coat the button with linseed oil
and allow it to dry slowly in a cool, ventilated place
(see pages 33–34).

3. You can also make square or hexagonal buttons,
and when you have had more practice, you can
carve patterns onto them, too.

PENDANT

This pendant is made in exactly the same way as the buttons on page 108, but this time working on a forked branch to give the oblong shape.

Materials

- Fresh branch, 10–20cm (4–8in) long: choose a branch with a fork or side branch at one end from which the pendant can be carved.
- Hand or electric drill with 2–4mm bit.
- Saw, preferably with fine teeth.
- Sandpaper, grit number 80–240 (optional).
- Linseed oil.
- 1–1.5mm leather cord, about 70–90cm (28–35in) long.

1. Following the basic method for the buttons (see page 108), carve the oblong shape of the pendant from the fork/side branch end, aiming to produce a finished pendant that has a depth of about 1cm (⅜in). Before sawing off the pendant, drill a hole from the side through the narrow end (this is the top of the pendant). If you wish, smooth with sandpaper and oil the wood (see pages 32–34).

2. To make the necklace as shown using adjustable sliding knots, first measure the length of the cord so that it is 1.5 times the circumference of your head. Thread the pendant onto the cord and arrange the cord ends so that they are parallel and at opposite sides. Tie a sliding knot at each side (see the illustrations above and below). Pull the cords to tighten or loosen the necklace.

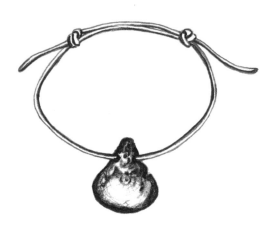

CORK DECORATIONS

Carved figures such as elves, birds or bears can be used to decorate corks, or you can make up your own design.

Materials
- Fresh branch, the same width as the cork.
- Sandpaper, grit number 80–240 (optional).
- Linseed oil (optional).
- Hand or electric drill with 5mm drill bit.
- Short piece of 5mm dowelling.
- Bottle cork.
- Wood glue.

··

1. Carve the desired figure (see Elf 2, page 68, Bear, page 80 and Bird, page 82, for some ideas and whittling guidance). Sand and seal it, if desired (see pages 32–34). Drill a hole in the top of the cork and in the bottom of the carved figure.

2. Put glue in both holes and insert the dowelling to join the cork and the figure together (see the illustration right).

WHITTLING KNIFE AND SHEATH

Here's an easy way to make your own whittling knife and a simple sheath to protect the blade made from birch bark.

Materials

- Piece of fresh branch, 9–12cm (3½ x 4¾in) long and 2.5–3cm (1–1⅛in) thick, or a piece of dry wood of the same size.
- Drill (preferably a drill stand) with drill bit matching the depth of the tang (the part of the knife that fits into the handle).
- Drill saw rasp.
- Saw or bench grinder (optional).
- Knife blade with short tang.
- Two-part epoxy adhesive.
- Linseed oil (optional).
- Sandpaper, grit number 80–240 (optional).

WHITTLING KNIFE

1. Shape the branch into a handle that feels comfortable
in your hand. It should be thicker in the middle than
at the ends. The handle does not need to be round
in shape, but can be oblong, or triangular, in which
case the broadest part is held uppermost (see the
illustration below).

2. Carefully drill two or three holes in the handle where the
tang is to be fixed to make a channel in which the width
of the tang can be set. Use a drill saw rasp to adjust the
depth of the hole to fit the tang. It may be difficult to get
right down inside the hole, and, if so, an adult may have
to shorten the tang by sawing a piece off or grinding it
using a bench grinder.

Knife blade showing a short
tang set in a handle.

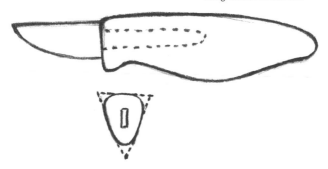

Cross-section of a handle.

3. Fix the knife blade firmly in place with the glue. (If the wood is fresh, it will shrink when it dries, and this may be enough to hold the knife blade firmly in place, but it is safest to use glue as well for added strength.)

4. Treat with oil if you wish; rub the oil into the wood with sandpaper to make the surface more resistant to wear and tear (see page 33–34).

WHITTLING SHEAF

Materials
- Birch bark.
- Corrugated cardboard (optional).
- Tape (optional).

. . . .

1. Cut a strip of birch bark to size, so that the length is about five times the knife blade length, and the width is the same as the knife blade width plus 1cm (⅜in).

2. Cut a binding strip from the birch bark about 5–10cm (2–4in) wide (depending on your preferred finished width) and 30–60cm (12–24in) long (depending on the length of the sheath required to house your knife). Cut each end of the binding strip to a point.

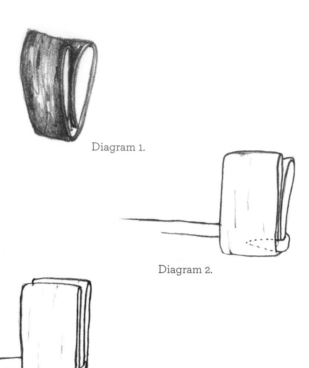

Diagram 1.

Diagram 2.

Diagram 3.

Diagram 4.

3. Fold the strip of bark for the sheath in half, with the underside of the bark facing out, then fold the two halves towards the centre (see diagram 1). Bind the sheath together: insert the pointed end of the binding strip between the bark (see diagram 2), then wrap the strip alternately outside and in between the bark layers (see diagrams 3 and 4).

Alternative method: You can make a simple sheath by rolling a piece of corrugated cardboard around the knife halfway up the handle and sticking tape round the cardboard to secure it in place.

FLOWER

This project is quick to do, but the work involved is fine and needs to be well controlled.

Materials
· Fresh elder branch, 10–20cm (4–8in) long and 1–1.5cm (³⁄₈–⁵⁄₈in) thick (the bark should be brownish; branches with fresh green bark cannot be used). Ensure there are no nodes on the 5cm (2in) section of branch that will form the flower.
· Thin twig for the stalk, 10–20cm (4–8in) long and 3–4mm (about ⅛in) thick

· ·

1. Neaten the end of the elder branch using simple cuts (this will become the underside of the flower). Scrape off the bark from 4–5cm (1½–2in) section at the neatened end by placing the knife blade horizontally against the branch and scraping away from yourself. This will become your flower. Do not cut into the branch.

2. Starting about 4cm (1½in) from the end of the branch, carve a thin sliver of wood finishing about 1cm (³⁄₈in) from the end of the branch to form the first petal, gently bending it out from the branch with your knife and taking great care not to cut it off! When you have raised it slightly, you will be able to curve it a little more with your fingers. Continue making petals, one after the

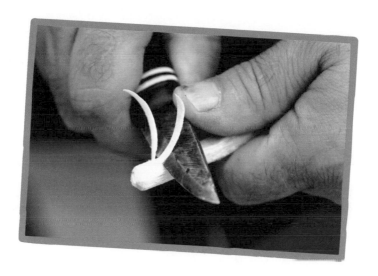

other all the way around (see photograph, above). Make two or more rounds of petals (see the photograph on pages 126–127).

3. If you have cut close to the pith, you will be able to simply break off the flower from the branch, otherwise cut it off carefully.

4. Push a thin twig into the pith on the underside of the flower to form a stalk. Bend the petals gently so they open out wide, or leave your flower partly open.

5. Trim off the end of the remaining branch and you are ready to begin carving the next flower.

GAMES

. . . .

Playing games is always fun, but there is
something extra special about playing them
using items you have made yourself. Here are
three games to try.

QUOITS

This well-known game is often played in the garden, so what could be better than to make this version with materials *from* the garden.

Materials
- Five pieces of fresh branch for the pegs, 30–35cm (12–14in) long and 2–3cm (³⁄₄–1¹⁄₈in) thick.
- Three flexible branches for the rings, such as willow twigs, about 1m (1yd) long.

1. To make the pegs, round off the five branches at one end and sharpen the other end to a point.

2. If you wish, you can decorate the pegs by carving figures at the top.

3. Beginning at the rounded end, cut rings or notches in the bark 2–2.5cm (³⁄₄–1in) apart: make two pegs with just two rings, two pegs with three rings and one peg with five rings.

4. Weave the willow twigs into three rings about 15cm (6in) in diameter, and you are ready to begin the game.

Play the game

Push or hammer the pegs into the lawn; the peg with five rings
should be in the centre and the others arranged in a square around it.
The players take turns to throw the willow rings over the pegs. Each
person has three goes each, winning 20 points if they land over the
pegs with two rings, 30 points for the pegs with three rings and 50
points for the peg in the middle.

MOUSE GAME

This game is all about being quick and alert,
and is played with tiny carved mice.

Materials

- Fresh branch, 10-20cm (4-8in) long (includes extra to hold while whittling), about 1.5cm (⅝in) thick.
- Hand or electric drill with 1.5-2mm drill bit or thin gimlet.
- Wood glue.
- Strong sewing thread (button thread).
- Matches.
- Dice cup and dice.
- Paper and pencil.

....

1. To make a mouse, begin by carving the underside of the branch flat and whittle a small nose at one end of the branch (see Mouse, page 78). The mouse should be about 2-3cm (¾ 1⅛in) long. As it is so small, it is best to carve the mouse's bottom while it is still attached to the branch and before cutting it off.

2. Bore a hole about 5mm (¼in) deep into the rear end of the mouse. Glue one end of a piece of thread 20-30cm (8-12in) long and insert it into the hole. Cut a match to a point, jam it into the hole alongside the thread and break it off as close to the hole as possible; this 'plug' will ensure that the tail stays firmly in place, helping it to withstand the rigours of the game. If you like, you can give the mouse some ears (see Mouse, page 78).

3. Make a minimum of six mice for the maximum number of players.

Note: it is good to have extra mice, in case a tail does come off in the heat of battle.)

Play the game (for 3–6 players)

On a piece of paper, draw a circle around the dice cup, making sure that the circle is big enough to cover several mice at once. Give one player the dice cup and dice, and give the others a mouse each. The mice are placed inside the circle, with the players holding onto their tails. The player with the dice cup then throws the dice, lifting the dice cup quickly to reveal the number thrown. If it is a 1 or a 6, the player must try to catch the mice in the circle with the cup by bringing it down over the mice as quickly as possible, while the other players must pull their mice out of the circle as quickly as possible to avoid being caught. The players take turns to throw the dice.

Count your points

You can choose whether to play a certain number of rounds, say three or more, or until one player has lost a certain number of points. Points are lost as follows:

- If your mouse is caught when a 1 or a 6 is thrown, you lose a point.
- If you pull your mouse out when a number between 2 and 5 is thrown, you lose a point.
- If the player with the dice cup tries to catch mice in the circle when a number between 2 and 5 is thrown, he or she loses a point.

Note: If you are the dice thrower, you are allowed to *pretend* you are going to catch the mice, even if you have not thrown a 1 or a 6, and players, you can also *pretend* you are going to pull your mouse out, as a nervous twitch may make someone else pull his or her mouse out, even if a 1 or a 6 has not been thrown.

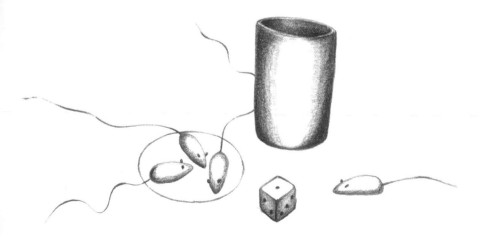

CHESS

Here is an easy way to make a chess set, including a leather chessboard that doubles up as a storage bag to keep the pieces in.

Materials
- Fresh branches with bark that is dark, but not too thick, long enough to allow for an extra piece to hold when whittling, 10–30cm (4–12in) and 2–2.5cm (¾–1in) thick.
- A piece of thin leather, large enough to make a circle with a diameter of about 64cm (25in).
- Two pencils and piece of string.
- Scissors.
- Dark leather paint and fine paintbrush.
- Dubbin and silicone spray (optional).
- Single hole punch.
- 1.5mm leather or knotting cord, 2m (2⅛yd) long.

....

1. I have chosen to make simple figures, leaving the bark on for one set of pieces and sanding smooth for the other (see the photographs on pages 138–139). The pawns are about 3cm (1⅛in) high, the king and queen about 5cm (2in) and the knights about 4cm (1½in). The two sets of pieces could also be differentiated by using light and dark woods, such as birch or hazel for the light pieces and laburnum for the dark.

1. To make the chessboard, start by marking out a circle
onto the rough (wrong) side of the leather: tie a pencil
to each end of a piece of string so that the length of the
string between the pencils measures 32cm (12½in). Place
the leather smooth side facing down and place the point
of one pencil at its centre; extend the string fully and
draw a circle on the rough side of the leather with the
other pencil. Cut out the circle with scissors.

3. Draw two lines 32cm (12in) long crossing at right angles in the centre of the leather circle (still smooth side down). Starting from where the lines cross, draw the chessboard with squares measuring 4 x 4cm (1½ x 1½in). There should be eight rows of eight squares. Paint alternate squares using dark leather paint with a fine paintbrush. To protect the leather, treat the smooth side with dubbin and the rough side with a silicone spray.

4. Punch holes all the way around the leather circle, 1–2cm (⅜–¾in) in from the edge and about 5cm (2in) apart, making sure that there are an even number of holes. Thread the leather cord in and out of the holes, starting from the outside. The leather can now be drawn together to form a bag to contain the chess pieces, and then opened out again when you are ready to play.

SUPPLIERS

Author's website and Etsy shop
www.snittesiden.dk
www.etsy.com/shop/Whittlingsale

Wood and whittling tools suppliers

UK
Isca Woodcrafts www.iscawoodcrafts.co.uk
G&S Specialist Timber www.toolsandtimber.co.uk
Classic Hand Tools www.classichandtools.com
The Toolpost www.toolpost.co.uk
Ockenden Timber www.ockenden-timber.co.uk

USA
Smoky Mountain Woodcarvers www.woodcarvers.com
Traditional Woodworker www.traditionalwoodworkercom.com
Wood Carvers Supply www.woodcarverssupply.com
Treeline www.treelineusa.com

Whittling and carving organisations and other whittlers
British Woodcarvers' Association
www.britishwoodcarversassociation.com
The Bird Whittler www.thebirdwhittler.co.uk
Nick's Birds www.nicksbirds.com
Nicke Helldorff www.handochtanke.se
Tom Nilsson www.tomtrasnidare.com
Vesa Jussila www.naturdiorama.se

INDEX

ABOUT THE AUTHOR

Frank Egholm is the father of five boys and has taught for 20 years at a school in Denmark; teaching has also been a source of inspiration for the many ideas in his craft books. He is the founder of Denmark's annual whittling festival.